TENNESSEE

Sarah Tieck

Big Buddy BOOKS
Explore the United States

VISIT US AT
www.abdopublishing.com

Published by ABDO Publishing Company, PO Box 398166, Minneapolis, MN 55439.

Copyright © 2013 by Abdo Consulting Group, Inc. International copyrights reserved in all countries. No part of this book may be reproduced in any form without written permission from the publisher. Big Buddy Books™ is a trademark and logo of ABDO Publishing Company.

Printed in the United States of America, North Mankato, Minnesota.
052012
092012

PRINTED ON RECYCLED PAPER

Coordinating Series Editor: Rochelle Baltzer
Contributing Editors: Megan M. Gunderson, Marcia Zappa
Graphic Design: Adam Craven
Cover Photograph: *Shutterstock*: KennStilger47.
Interior Photographs/Illustrations: *AP Photo*: Cal Sport Media via AP Images (p. 27), Frank Micelotta/PictureGroup via AP IMAGES (p. 25), North Wind Picture Archives via AP Images (pp. 13, 23), Wade Payne (p. 27); *Getty Images*: Fred A. Sabine/NBC/NBCU Photo Bank via Getty Images (p. 25); *Glow Images*: Imagebroker RM (p. 17), JTB Photo (p. 26); *iStockphoto*: ©iStockphoto.com/JimmyAnderson (p. 19), ©iStockphoto.com/BasieB (p. 30), ©iStockphoto.com/Davel5957 (p. 9), ©iStockphoto.com/MaryBB (p. 21), ©iStockphoto.com/DenisTangneyJr (p. 11); *Shutterstock*: Steve Byland (p. 30), Creative Jen Designs (p. 26), David Davis (p. 27), Brian Dunne (p. 19), Melinda Fawver (p. 11), Inna Felker (p. 30), Philip Lange (p. 30), Geir Olav Lyngfjell (p. 5), Harris Shiffman (p. 29), skphotography (p. 9).

All population figures taken from the 2010 US census.

Library of Congress Cataloging-in-Publication Data

Tieck, Sarah, 1976-
  Tennessee / Sarah Tieck.
    p. cm. -- (Explore the United States)
  ISBN 978-1-61783-381-6
  1. Tennessee--Juvenile literature. I. Title.
  F436.3.T54 2013
  976.8--dc23
                              2012017230

TENNESSEE

Contents

ONE NATION

The United States is a **diverse** country. It has farmland, cities, coasts, and mountains. Its people come from many different backgrounds. And, its history covers more than 200 years.

Today the country includes 50 states. Tennessee is one of these states. Let's learn more about Tennessee and its story!

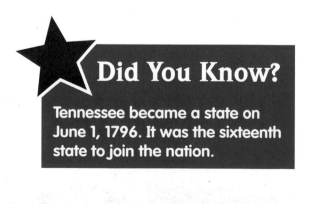

Did You Know?

Tennessee became a state on June 1, 1796. It was the sixteenth state to join the nation.

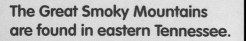

The Great Smoky Mountains
are found in eastern Tennessee.

TENNESSEE UP CLOSE

The United States has four main **regions**. Tennessee is in the South.

Tennessee has eight states on its borders. Kentucky and Virginia are north. North Carolina is east. Georgia, Alabama, and Mississippi are south. Arkansas and Missouri are west.

Tennessee has a total area of 42,145 square miles (109,155 sq km). About 6.3 million people live there.

REGIONS OF THE UNITED STATES

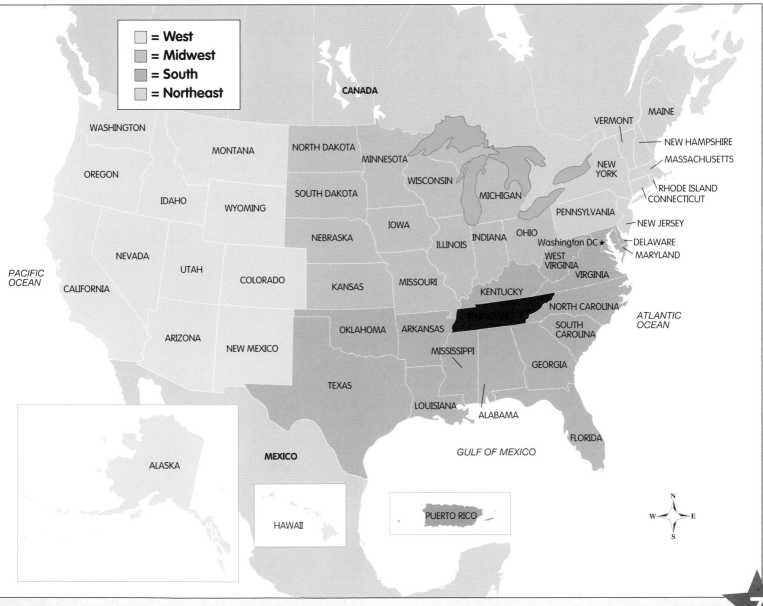

= West
= Midwest
= South
= Northeast

CANADA

WASHINGTON

MONTANA

NORTH DAKOTA

MINNESOTA

VERMONT

MAINE

NEW HAMPSHIRE

MASSACHUSETTS

OREGON

WISCONSIN

NEW YORK

RHODE ISLAND
CONNECTICUT

IDAHO

SOUTH DAKOTA

MICHIGAN

PENNSYLVANIA

WYOMING

IOWA

OHIO

NEW JERSEY

NEVADA

NEBRASKA

ILLINOIS

INDIANA

Washington DC ★

DELAWARE
MARYLAND

WEST VIRGINIA

PACIFIC OCEAN

UTAH

COLORADO

KANSAS

MISSOURI

KENTUCKY

VIRGINIA

CALIFORNIA

ARIZONA

NEW MEXICO

OKLAHOMA

ARKANSAS

TENNESSEE

NORTH CAROLINA

ATLANTIC OCEAN

SOUTH CAROLINA

MISSISSIPPI

TEXAS

GEORGIA

LOUISIANA

ALABAMA

FLORIDA

GULF OF MEXICO

ALASKA

MEXICO

HAWAII

PUERTO RICO

N
W   E
S

7

IMPORTANT CITIES

Memphis is Tennessee's largest city. It is home to 646,889 people. It is located on the Mississippi River. Many people visit Memphis to experience barbecued food and blues music.

Tennessee

Nashville ★

● Knoxville

● Memphis

The Wolf River (*left*) flows into the Mississippi River near downtown Memphis.

Beale Street is a famous Memphis street. It is known for live blues music.

Nashville is Tennessee's **capital**. It is also the second-largest city in the state. It is home to 601,222 people. Nashville is known for country music. The Grand Ole Opry House and the Country Music Hall of Fame and Museum are located there.

Knoxville is the state's third-largest city, with 178,874 people. It is home to the University of Tennessee. Also, it is close to Great Smoky Mountains National Park.

The Shelby Street Bridge crosses over the Cumberland River in Nashville.

Knoxville is one of the largest cities in the Great Smoky Mountains area.

TENNESSEE IN HISTORY

Tennessee's history includes Native Americans, explorers, and settlers. Native Americans hunted and farmed in present-day Tennessee for thousands of years.

Spanish explorers visited what is now Tennessee in 1540. The first English explorers came in the 1670s. By 1770, settlers had arrived. They worked hard to build towns. Tennessee became the sixteenth state on June 1, 1796.

Daniel Boone was a famous pioneer. In 1775, he explored parts of what is now Tennessee.

Timeline

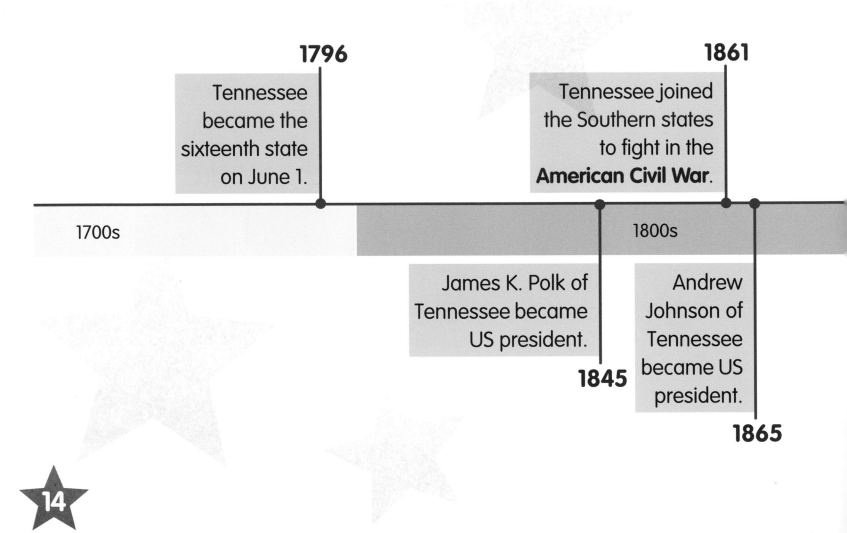

1796

Tennessee became the sixteenth state on June 1.

1861

Tennessee joined the Southern states to fight in the **American Civil War**.

1700s

1800s

James K. Polk of Tennessee became US president.

1845

Andrew Johnson of Tennessee became US president.

1865

1933

The US government established the Tennessee Valley Authority. Its job was to control floods and produce electricity.

1968

Civil rights leader Martin Luther King Jr. was shot and killed in Memphis.

2005

The *Grand Ole Opry* celebrated 80 years. It is country music's longest-running radio show. It is recorded at Nashville's Opry House.

1900s

2000s

In Oak Ridge, US government scientists began working to create the first **atomic bomb**.

Knoxville hosted the World's Fair.

Record-setting floods harmed Tennessee, including parts of Memphis and Nashville.

1942

1982

2010

ACROSS THE LAND

Tennessee has mountains, valleys, rivers, and forests. The Mississippi River forms the state's western border. The Blue Ridge Mountains are in eastern Tennessee.

Many types of animals make their homes in the state. These include deer, ducks, beavers, and rabbits.

Did You Know?

In July, the average temperature in Tennessee is 78°F (26°C). In January, it is 38°F (3°C).

★★★

Clingmans Dome is the highest point in Tennessee. It is 6,643 feet (2,025 m) tall. There, an observation tower lets people see Great Smoky Mountains National Park.

Earning a Living

Tennessee has many important businesses. People work in service jobs, such as shipping goods and helping visitors. The state's manufacturing companies make foods, beverages, and computer parts.

Tennessee has many natural **resources**. Its mines produce coal, sand, and cement. Its farmers grow corn, cotton, and soybeans. Farmers also raise livestock.

FedEx Corporation is a large company based in Memphis. It ships goods around the world.

Beef cattle and chickens are raised on Tennessee's farms.

Natural Wonder

The Great Smoky Mountains are part of the Blue Ridge mountain chain. They are covered in thick forests.

Great Smoky Mountains National Park includes much of the mountains. It covers more than 800 square miles (2,100 sq km) of land in Tennessee and North Carolina. It is one of the most popular US national parks. People fish, camp, hike, and ride horses in the park.

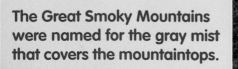

The Great Smoky Mountains were named for the gray mist that covers the mountaintops.

21

HOMETOWN HEROES

Many famous people are from Tennessee. Davy Crockett was born in eastern Tennessee in 1786.

Crockett became known for hunting and fighting in the wild. He worked for the Tennessee and US governments. He fought in the war for Texas independence in the 1830s. Sadly, Crockett was killed in one of its most famous battles at the Alamo.

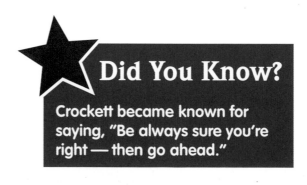

Did You Know?

Crockett became known for saying, "Be always sure you're right — then go ahead."

Many people consider Crockett a hero. There are lots of stories about his adventures!

Aretha Franklin was born in Memphis in 1942. She grew up in Detroit, Michigan. She became known for singing at her father's church.

Franklin was a popular singer in the late 1960s and early 1970s. One of her most famous songs is "Respect."

Franklin was known for her style and music in the late 1960s. She sang a type of music called soul.

Franklin is called "the Queen of Soul." Over the years, she has received many awards and honors for her work.

Tour Book

Do you want to go to Tennessee? If you visit the state, here are some places to go and things to do!

★ Listen

Take in some country music! The famous Grand Ole Opry House is one place to hear well-known singers, such as Taylor Swift and Carrie Underwood! People take tours and see live shows there.

★ Remember

Visit rock-and-roll star Elvis Presley's Memphis home. It is named Graceland. There, people can see his costumes and pay their respects at his grave.

★ Cheer

See a University of Tennessee at Knoxville game. The school is known for its men's football and women's basketball teams.

★ Play

Visit Dollywood in Pigeon Forge. The park is owned by famous country singer Dolly Parton. It is known for rides and music shows.

★ Discover

Spend time at Cades Cove. This part of Great Smoky Mountains National Park features scenery, animals, and historic homes and buildings. You can see a working mill at the Cable Mill historic area.

A GREAT STATE

The story of Tennessee is important to the United States. The people and places that make up this state offer something special to the country. Together with all the states, Tennessee helps make the United States great.

Lookout Mountain rises above the Tennessee River. Northern civil war soldiers won the Battle Above the Clouds there in 1863.

Fast Facts

Date of Statehood:
June 1, 1796

Population (rank):
6,346,105
(17th most-populated state)

Total Area (rank):
42,145 square miles
(35th largest state)

Motto:
"Agriculture and Commerce"

Nickname:
Volunteer State

State Capital:
Nashville

Flag:

Flower: Iris

Postal Abbreviation:
TN

Tree: Tulip Tree

Bird: Northern Mockingbird

30

Important Words

American Civil War the war between the Northern and Southern states from 1861 to 1865.

atomic bomb a bomb that uses the energy of atoms. Atoms are tiny particles that make up matter.

capital a city where government leaders meet.

civil rights the rights of a citizen, such as the right to vote or freedom of speech.

diverse made up of things that are different from each other.

region a large part of a country that is different from other parts.

resource a supply of something useful or valued.

Web Sites

To learn more about Tennessee, visit ABDO Publishing Company online. Web sites about Tennessee are featured on our Book Links page. These links are routinely monitored and updated to provide the most current information available.

www.abdopublishing.com

Index

1840